alfred's max

Guitar 1

MW00378371

see it • hear it • play it

RON MANUS
L. C. HARNSBERGER

Alfred's MAX™ is the next best thing to having your own private teacher. No confusion, no frustration, no guesswork—just lessons that are well paced and easy to follow. You listen to the music you're learning to play and watch a professional show how it's done, then get time to stretch out and put it all together. No matter how you like to learn, Alfred's MAX™ series gives you the ultimate learning experience at a screamin' deal of a price.

Cover photos: Martin D-28 guitar courtesy of Martin Guitar Company.
Electric guitar courtesy of Daisy Rock Guitars, photograph by Karen Miller.

Alfred

CONTENTS

The Parts of the Guitar 3
Steel Strings and Nylon Strings

How to Hold Your Guitar 4

The Right Hand 5
Strumming with a Pick
Strumming with Your Fingers

The Left Hand 6
Proper Left-Hand Position
Placing a Finger on a String
How to Read Chord Diagrams

Tuning Your Guitar 7
Using the DVD
Tuning the Guitar to Itself
Pitch Pipes and Electronic Tuners

The Basics of Reading Music 8
The Staff
The Treble Clef
Measures (Bars)

Notes on the First String E 9
Playing E, F and G on My Extra Fine Guitar
Once Again
Extra Credit

Counting Time 11
Four Kinds of Notes
Time Signatures

Notes on the Second String B 12
Jammin' on Two Strings
Up Two Flights
Beautiful Brown Eyes
Rockin' Guitar

Jingle Bells 15

Notes on the Third String G 16
Jammin' on Three Strings
Au Clair de la Lune
Largo from the New World Symphony

Repeat Signs 18
Aura Lee

Chords 20
Two-Note Exercise
Three-Note Chord Exercise

Three-String C Chord 21
Ode to Joy

Three-String G7 Chord 22
Jammin' with Two Chords
Love Somebody

Three-String G Chord 24
She'll Be Comin' 'Round the Mountain
Down in the Valley

Notes on the Fourth String D 26
Old MacDonald Had a Farm
Reuben Reuben
C Blues

Merry Widow Waltz 28

Daisy Bell 29

Four-String G & G7 Chords 30
Rock Me Mozart!

Notes on the Fifth String A 32
Volga Boatmen
Peter Gray
A Minor Boogie

Liebesträum 34

High A 35
Back in Russia
The Riddle Song

Incomplete Measures 37
A-Tisket, A-Tasket
The Yellow Rose of Texas

Notes on the Sixth String E 39
All the Notes You've Learned So Far

Tempo Signs 40
Three-Tempo Rock
1812 Overture
Theme from Carmen

Bass-Chord Accompaniment 41
Can-Can (duet)

Dynamics 43
Theme from Beethoven's Fifth Symphony

Half Rests & Whole Rests 44
The Desert Song
Echo Rock

Four-String C Chord 45

Ties 45
Shenandoah

When the Saints Go Marching In
(duet or trio) 46

Guitar Fingerboard Chart 47

Certificate of Promotion 48

About the DVD

The DVD contains valuable demonstrations of all the instructional material in the book. You will get the best results by following along with your book as you watch these video segments. Musical examples that are not performed with video are included as audio tracks on the DVD for listening and playing along.

THE PARTS OF THE GUITAR

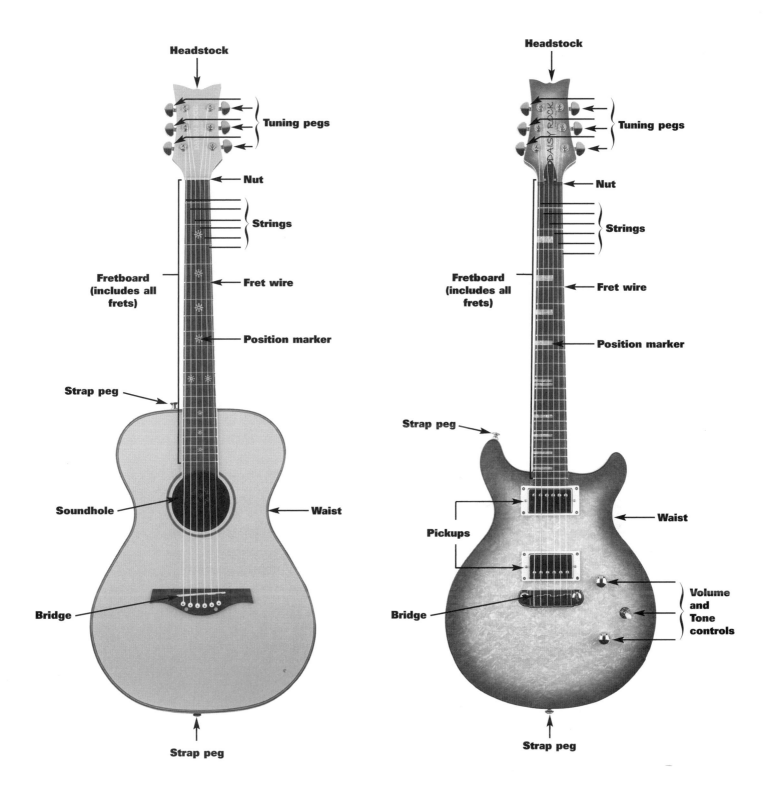

Steel Strings and Nylon Strings

Steel strings are found on both acoustic and electric guitars.
They have a bright and brassy sound.

Nylon strings are usually found on classical and flamenco guitars.
They have a mellow, delicate sound. Nylon strings are often easier for
beginners to play because they are easier on the fingers than steel strings.

HOW TO HOLD YOUR GUITAR

Below are three ways to hold your guitar.
Pick the one that is most comfortable for you.

When playing, keep your left wrist away from the fingerboard. This will allow your fingers to be in a better position to finger the chords. Press your fingers firmly, but make certain they do not touch the neighboring strings.

Sitting.

Sitting with legs crossed.

Standing with strap.

THE RIGHT HAND

To *strum* means to play the strings with your right hand by brushing quickly across them. There are two common ways of strumming the strings. One is with a pick, and the other is with your fingers.

Strumming with a Pick

Hold the pick between your thumb and index finger. Hold it firmly, but don't squeeze it too hard.

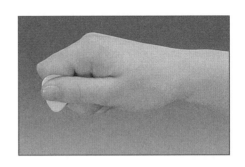

Strum from the sixth string (the thickest, lowest-sounding string) to the first string (the thinnest, highest-sounding string).

Start near the top string.

Move mostly your wrist, not just your arm. Finish near the bottom string.

Important:
Strum by mostly moving your wrist, not just your arm. Use as little motion as possible. Start as close to the top string as you can, and never let your hand move past the edge of the guitar.

Strumming with Your Fingers

First, decide if you feel more comfortable strumming with the side of your thumb or the nail of your index finger. The strumming motion is the same with the thumb or finger as it is when using the pick. Strum from the sixth string (the thickest, lowest-sounding string) to the first string (the thinnest, highest-sounding string).

Strumming with the thumb.

Strumming with the index finger.

Here is a great exercise to get used to strumming.

Let's Strum

Strum all six strings slowly and evenly. Count your strums out loud as you play.
Repeat this exercise until you feel comfortable strumming the strings.

	strum	strum	strum	strum	strum	strum	strum	strum
	/	/	/	/	/	/	/	/
Count:	1	2	3	4	5	6	7	8

THE LEFT HAND

Proper Left-Hand Position

Learning to use your left-hand fingers starts with a good hand position. Place your hand so your thumb rests comfortably in the middle of the back of the neck. Position your fingers on the front of the neck as if you are gently squeezing a ball between them and your thumb. Keep your elbow in and your fingers curved.

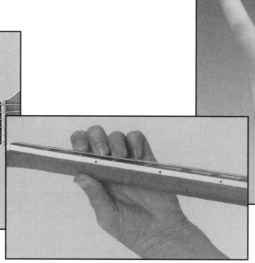

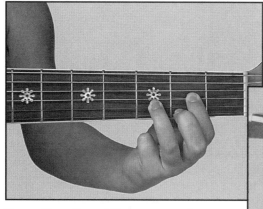

Keep elbow in and fingers curved.

Like gently squeezing a ball between your fingertips and thumb.

Placing a Finger on a String

When you press a string with a left-hand finger, make sure you press firmly with the tip of your finger and as close to the fret wire as you can without actually being right on it. Short fingernails are important! This will create a clean, bright tone.

RIGHT
Finger presses the string down near the fret without actually being on it.

WRONG
Finger is too far from fret wire; tone is "buzzy" and indefinite.

WRONG
Finger is on top of fret wire; tone is muffled and unclear.

How to Read Chord Diagrams

Fingering diagrams show where to place the fingers of your left hand. Strings that are not played are shown with a dashed line. The finger that is to be pressed down is shown as a circle with a number in it. The number indicates which finger is used. The diagram at the right shows the first finger on the first fret.

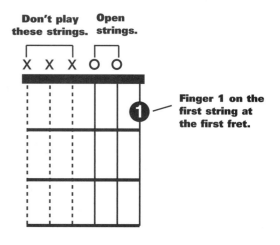

Don't play these strings.

Open strings.

Finger 1 on the first string at the first fret.

TUNING YOUR GUITAR

First, make sure your strings are wound properly around the tuning pegs. They should go from the inside to the outside as illustrated to the right. Some guitars have all six tuning pegs on the same side of the headstock. If this is the case, make sure all six strings are wound the same way, from the inside out.

Turning a tuning peg clockwise makes the pitch lower. Turning a tuning peg counter-clockwise makes the pitch higher. Be sure not to tune the strings too high because they could break.

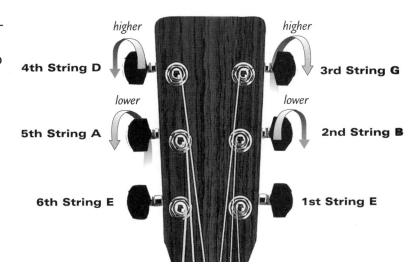

Important:

Always remember that the thinnest, highest-sounding string, the one closest to the floor, is the first string. The thickest, lowest-sounding string, the one closest to the ceiling, is the sixth string. When guitarists say "the highest string," they are referring to the highest-sounding string.

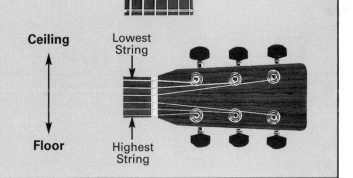

Using the DVD

When tuning while watching the DVD, listen to the directions and match each of your guitar's strings to the corresponding pitches on the DVD.

Tuning the Guitar to Itself

When your sixth string is in tune, you can tune the rest of the strings using the guitar alone. First, tune the sixth string to E on the piano:

Then, follow the instructions below to get the guitar in tune.

Press 5th fret of 6th string to get pitch of 5th string (A).

Press 5th fret of 5th string to get pitch of 4th string (D).

Press 5th fret of 4th string to get pitch of 3rd string (G).

Press 4th fret of 3rd string to get pitch of 2nd string (B).

Press 5th fret of 2nd string to get pitch of 1st string (E).

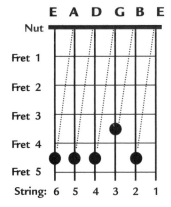

Pitch Pipes and Electronic Tuners

If you don't have a piano available, consider buying an electronic tuner or pitch pipe. There are many types available, and a salesperson at your local music store can help you decide which is best for you.

THE BASICS OF READING MUSIC

Musical sounds are indicated by symbols called *notes*.
Their time value is determined by their color (white or black)
and by stems or flags attached to the note.

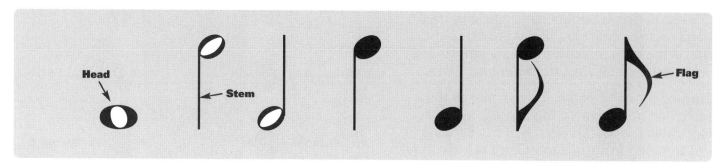

The Staff

The notes are named after the first seven letters of the alphabet (A–G), which are repeated
to embrace the entire range of musical sound. The name and pitch of a note are determined
by the note's position on five horizontal lines and four spaces between called the *staff*.

5th LINE
4th LINE   4th SPACE
3rd LINE   3rd SPACE
2nd LINE   2nd SPACE
1st LINE   1st SPACE

The Treble Clef

During the evolution of musical notation, the staff had from 2 to 20
lines, and symbols were invented to locate certain lines and the
pitch of the note on that line. These symbols were called *clefs*.

Music for the guitar is written in the *G clef* or *treble clef*. Originally the Gothic letter G
was used on a four-line staff to establish the pitch of G.

This grew into the modern symbol we use today:

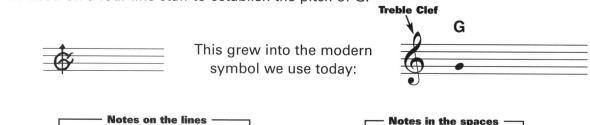

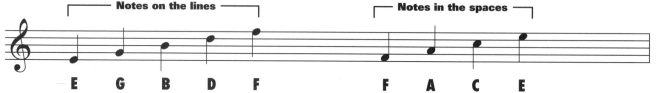

Measures (Bars)

Music is also divided into equal parts
called *measures* or *bars*. One measure
is divided from another by a *bar line*:

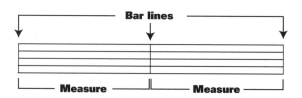

NOTES ON THE FIRST STRING E

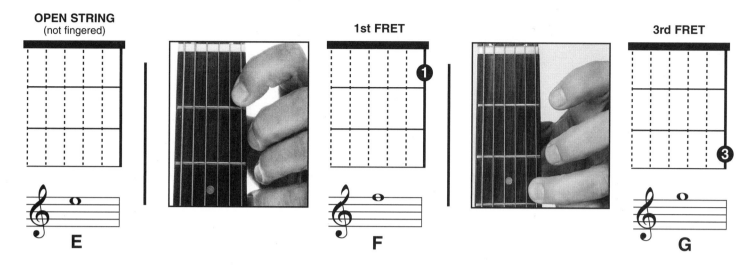

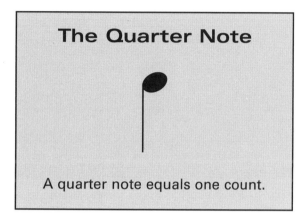

The Quarter Note

A quarter note equals one count.

Play this example slowly and evenly. Use down-strokes for all the music in this book.

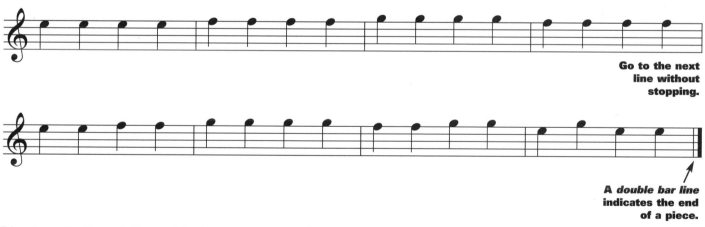

Go to the next line without stopping.

A *double bar line* indicates the end of a piece.

Playing E, F and G on My Extra Fine Guitar

Once Again

When you play the F on the 1st fret and follow it with the G on the 3rd fret, keep the first finger down. You will only hear the G, but when you go back to the F, it will sound smooth.

Extra Credit

Make sure to place your left-hand fingers as close to the fret wires as possible without touching them.

COUNTING TIME

Four Kinds of Notes

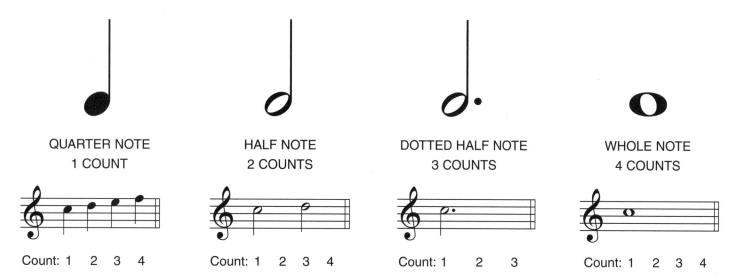

Time Signatures

Each piece of music has numbers at the beginning called a *time signature.*
These numbers tell us how to count time.

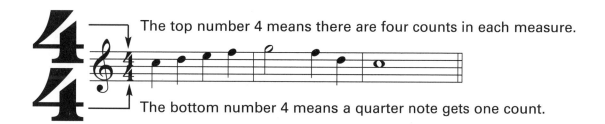

The top number 4 means there are four counts in each measure.

The bottom number 4 means a quarter note gets one count.

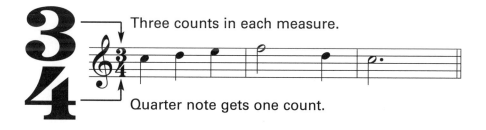

Three counts in each measure.

Quarter note gets one count.

IMPORTANT: Fill in the missing time signatures of the songs already learned.

NOTES ON THE SECOND STRING B

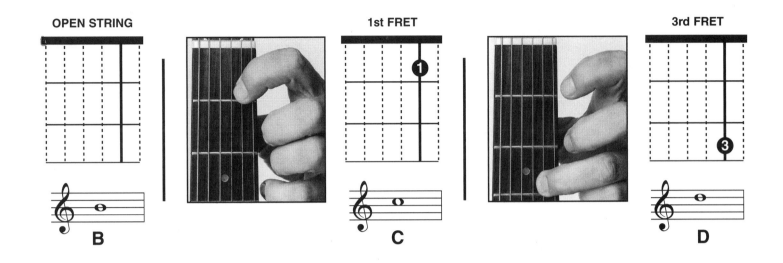

Count: 1   2   3   4   1   2   3   4   (etc.)

Jammin' on Two Strings

Count: 1   2   3   4   (etc.)

Up Two Flights

Count: 1   2   3   1   2   3   (etc.)

Beautiful Brown Eyes

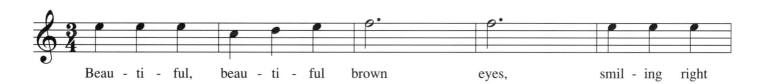

Beau - ti - ful,   beau - ti - ful   brown   eyes,   smil - ing   right

in - to   my   heart.   But   now   where   are   those   beau - ti - ful

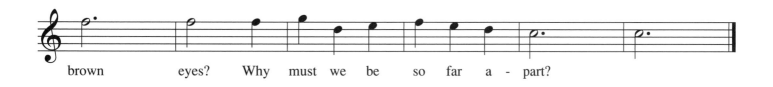

brown   eyes?   Why   must   we   be   so   far   a - part?

Rockin' Guitar

Letters called *chord symbols* that are placed above each staff may be used for a duet.
Either have a friend or teacher play the chords while you play the notes, or play along with the
audio tracks on the DVD. Many of the tunes in the rest of this book include chords for duets.

Eric Johnson is widely accepted as one of the most influential and gifted guitarists of the twentieth century. Born in Austin, Texas, he was only 16 when his immense talent was recognized, and by 21 he'd begun playing in legendary bands that came to include the Electromagnets, the Eric Johnson Group, and Avenue. After naming him Best Overall Guitarist for four consecutive years, *Guitar Player* magazine inducted him into their Gallery of Greats in 1995.

Jingle Bells

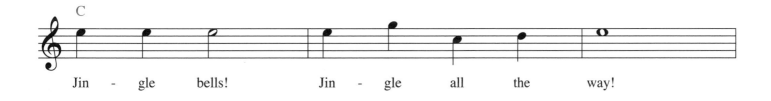

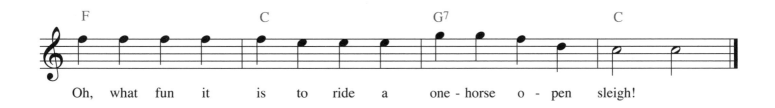

NOTES ON THE THIRD STRING G

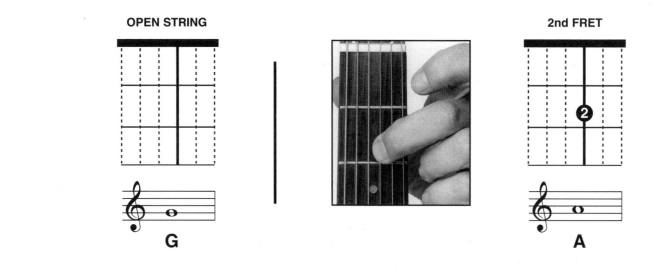

OPEN STRING

G

2nd FRET

A

Jammin' on Three Strings

Au Clair de la Lune

Largo

from the New World Symphony

Dvořák

REPEAT SIGNS

"Aura Lee" is an old American folk song that was later recorded by Elvis Presley and called "Love Me Tender." This music uses *repeat signs.* The double dots inside the double bars tell you that everything between those double bars is to be repeated.

Aura Lee

Dubbed the "King of Rock and Roll," Elvis Presley influenced several generations of young people to play guitar and may have had more impact on contemporary culture than any other figure in music.

CHORDS

A *chord* is a combination of three or more notes played at the same time.
All the notes are connected by a stem unless they are whole notes, which have no stem.
The stems can go either up or down.

Two-Note Exercise

This exercise will get you used to playing two notes at a time—open B and open E.
Play both strings together with one down-stroke.

Three-Note Chord Exercise

This is the first time you are playing three-note chords.
All the chords in this exercise are made up of the open G, B and E strings.
Play it with your wrist free and relaxed. Remember to keep your eyes on the notes and not your hands.

THREE-STRING C CHORD

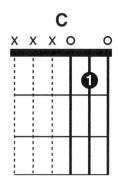

The Quarter Rest

It tells you to be silent for one count.

To make the rest very clear, stop the sound of the strings by touching the strings lightly with the heel of your right hand.

Ode to Joy

Theme from Beethoven's Ninth Symphony

Beethoven

THREE-STRING G⁷ CHORD

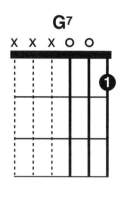

Jammin' with Two Chords

First, play the written notes and learn the melody, then play just the chords and sing.
The slanted lines following a chord symbol mean to play that same chord for each slash.
You repeat the same chord until a new chord symbol appears.

Love Somebody

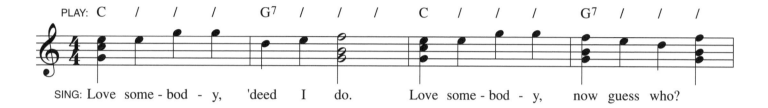

SING: Love some - bod - y, 'deed I do. Love some - bod - y, now guess who?

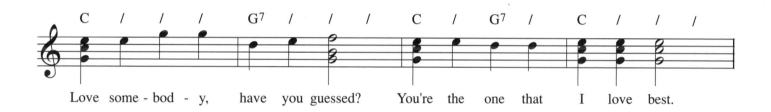

Love some - bod - y, have you guessed? You're the one that I love best.

Love some - bod - y, want to hear? Let me whis - per in your ear.

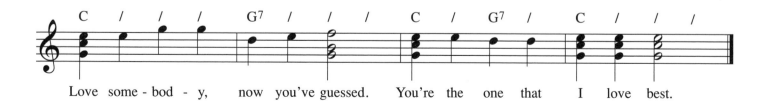

Love some - bod - y, now you've guessed. You're the one that I love best.

THREE-STRING G CHORD

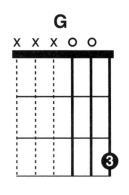

She'll Be Comin' 'Round the Mountain

First, play the written notes and learn the melody, then play just the chords and sing.

Down in the Valley

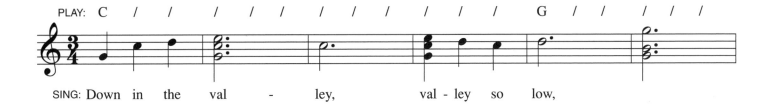

PLAY: C / / / / / / / / / / G / / / / /

SING: Down in the val - ley, val - ley so low,

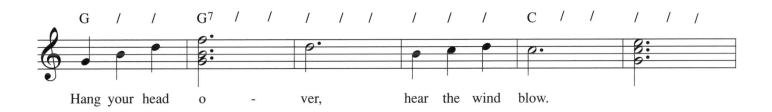

G / / G7 / / / / / / / / C / / / / /

Hang your head o - ver, hear the wind blow.

C / / / / / / / / / / G / / / / /

Ros - es love sun - shine, vio - lets love dew.

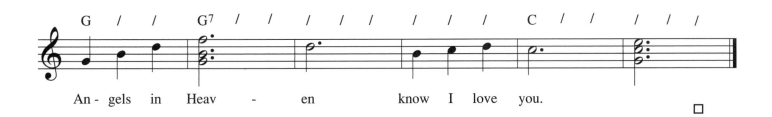

G / / G7 / / / / / / / / C / / / / /

An - gels in Heav - en know I love you.

NOTES ON THE FOURTH STRING D

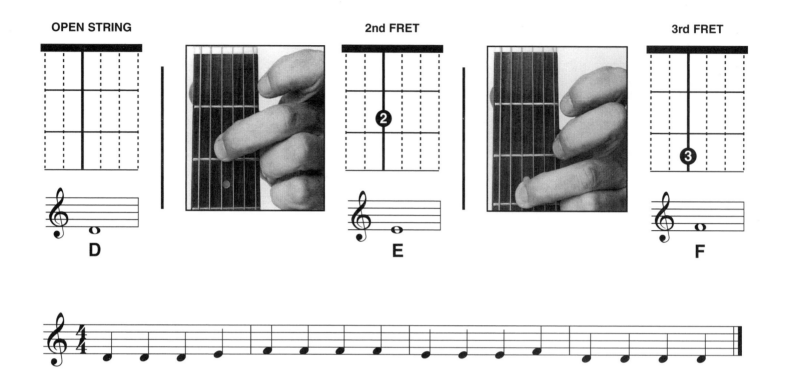

Old MacDonald Had a Farm

"Reuben Reuben" uses a *fermata* (), which is also called a *hold sign* or *pause sign*. This sign tells you to lengthen the value of the note (usually twice its normal value).

Reuben Reuben

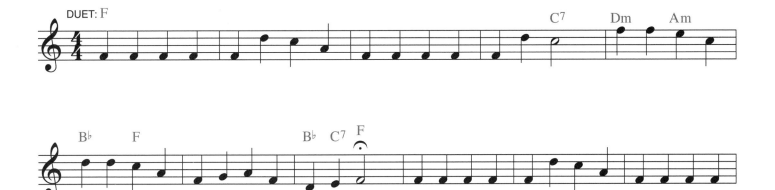

C Blues

C stands for *common time,* which is the same as $\frac{4}{4}$ time.

Merry Widow Waltz

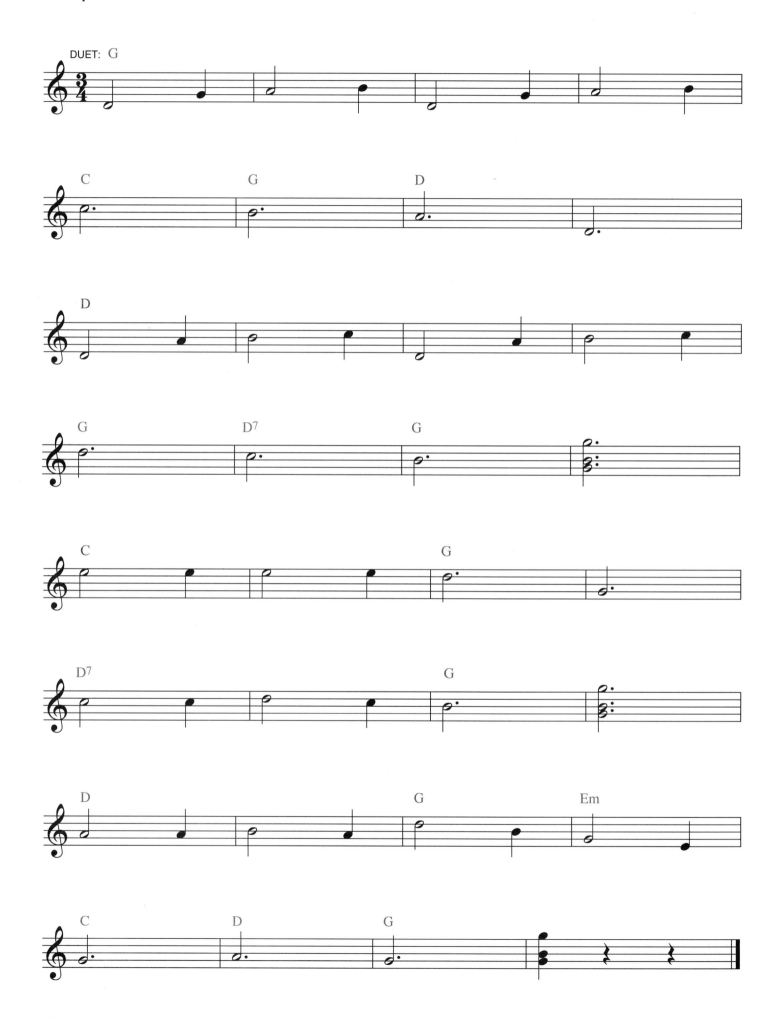

Now that you are getting better at playing chords, here is a song that will be lots of fun to play. In "Daisy Bell," you will be going from one note, to two notes, to three notes.

Daisy Bell

FOUR-STRING G & G⁷ CHORDS

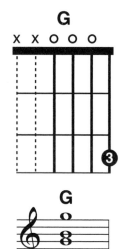
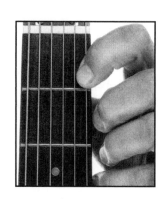
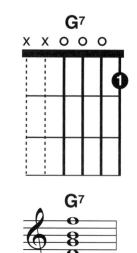

Although these new chords have the same names as chords you have already learned, they use four notes and sound more full.

Rock Me Mozart!

Mozart

With a penchant for outrageous stage antics like lighting his guitar on fire, Jimi Hendrix was one of the most influential guitarists of his generation. Though he lived only a short life, his place in history as one of rock's greatest legends is solidified by his amazing technique and brilliant songwriting.

NOTES ON THE FIFTH STRING A

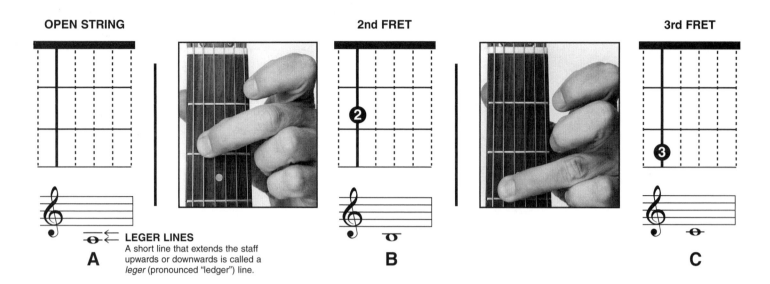

OPEN STRING

2nd FRET

3rd FRET

LEGER LINES
A short line that extends the staff upwards or downwards is called a *leger* (pronounced "ledger") line.

A

B

C

Volga Boatmen

DUET: Am   Dm   Am   Dm   Am

F   C   G   Am   Dm   Am

Peter Gray

A Minor Boogie

"Liebesträum" was written in 1845 by the famous composer Franz Liszt. The title means "love dream."

Liebesträum

Liszt

HIGH A

5th FRET

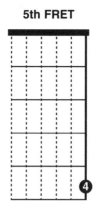

A

Back in Russia

First, play the written notes and learn the melody, then play just the chords and sing.

The Riddle Song

PLAY: C / / / (etc.)

SING: Gave my love a cher - ry that has no stone, I

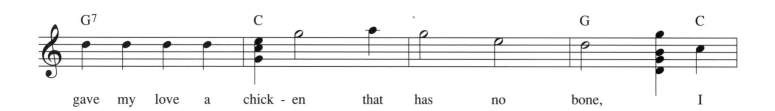

gave my love a chick - en that has no bone, I

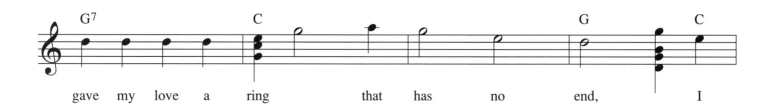

gave my love a ring that has no end, I

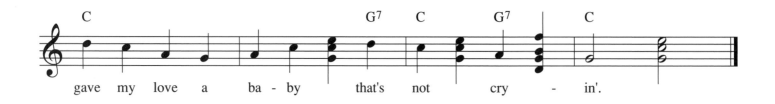

gave my love a ba - by that's not cry - in'.

INCOMPLETE MEASURES

Not all pieces of music begin on the first beat.
Sometimes, music begins with an incomplete measure called a *pickup*.
If the pickup is one beat, the last measure will only have three beats in $\frac{4}{4}$, or two beats in $\frac{3}{4}$.

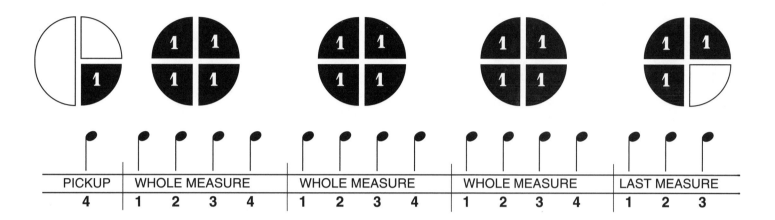

PICKUP	WHOLE MEASURE	WHOLE MEASURE	WHOLE MEASURE	LAST MEASURE
4	1 2 3 4	1 2 3 4	1 2 3 4	1 2 3

A-Tiskit, A-Tasket

The Yellow Rose of Texas

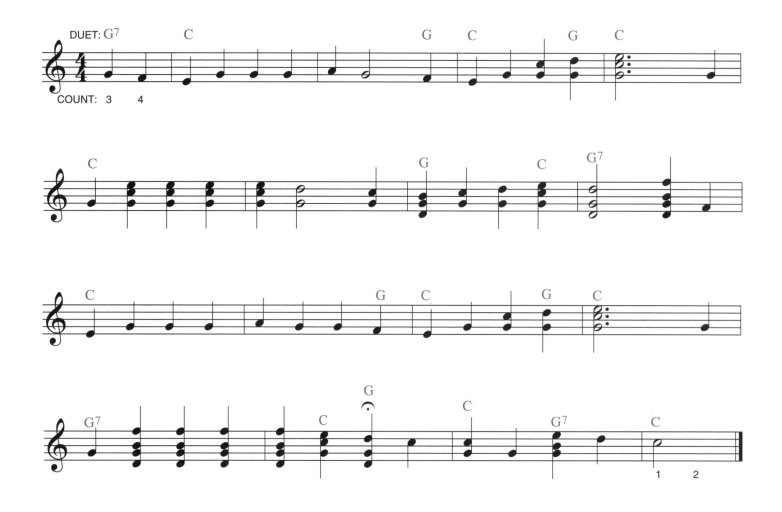

Texas guitarist Stevie Ray Vaughan brought the blues to an entire generation of music lovers and was admired by the likes of Eric Clapton, David Bowie and Buddy Guy for his extraordinary skill. Tragically, a plane crash claimed the life of this celebrated guitar legend in 1990.

Photo: Robert Knight

NOTES ON THE SIXTH STRING E

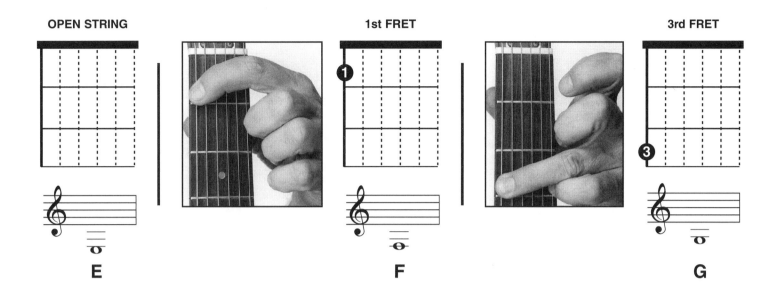

OPEN STRING   1st FRET   3rd FRET

E   F   G

All the Notes You've Learned So Far

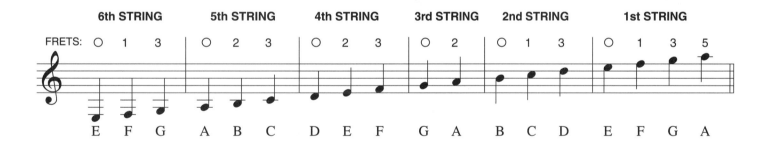

6th STRING	5th STRING	4th STRING	3rd STRING	2nd STRING	1st STRING
FRETS: ○ 1 3	○ 2 3	○ 2 3	○ 2	○ 1 3	○ 1 3 5

E F G   A B C   D E F   G A B   C D E   F G A

TEMPO SIGNS

A *tempo* sign tells you how fast to play music. The three most common tempo signs are below:

Andante (SLOW)   **Moderato** (MODERATELY)   **Allegro** (FAST)

Three-Tempo Rock

Play three times: 1st time **Andante**, 2nd time **Moderato**, 3rd time **Allegro**.

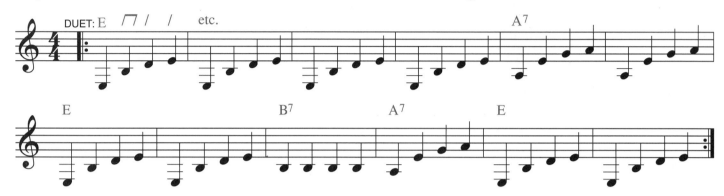

1812 Overture

Tchaikovsky

Theme from Carmen

Bizet

BASS-CHORD ACCOMPANIMENT

A great way to accompany songs is to break up chords by playing a single note followed by a smaller chord. You can take all the chords you have learned so far and create *bass-chord accompaniments.*

The easiest way is to play only the lowest note (called the *bass note*) on the 1st beat and then the rest of the chord on the 2nd, 3rd and 4th beats. That complete pattern is called **bass-chord-chord-chord**. A variation of this pattern repeats the bass note again on the 3rd beat for a **bass-chord-bass-chord** pattern. Here is an example that uses both patterns.

In "Can-Can," both a melody part and accompaniment part are written out. You can play with a friend, teacher or the DVD. Be sure to learn both parts.

Can-Can (duet)

Offenbach

Note: Part 2 is written in bass-chord-chord-chord style.
It can also be played in bass-chord-bass-chord style.

Since the early 1960s, songwriter and performer Bob Dylan has inspired countless fans of both folk music and rock 'n' roll with equal success.

DYNAMICS

Symbols that show how soft or loud to play are called *dynamics.* These symbols come from Italian words. The four most common dynamics are shown here:

p *(piano)* **SOFT** mf *(mezzo-forte)* **MODERATELY LOUD** f *(forte)* **LOUD** ff *(fortissimo)* **VERY LOUD**

Theme from Beethoven's Fifth Symphony

Allegro

Beethoven

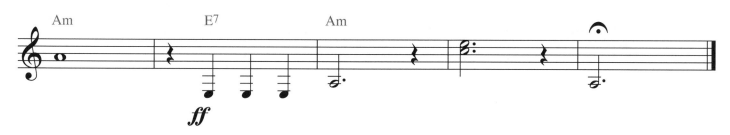

HALF RESTS & WHOLE RESTS

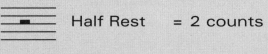

We already learned about a quarter rest equaling one beat.
Here are two more rests:

Half Rest = 2 counts

Whole Rest = 4 counts in $\frac{4}{4}$ time
= 3 counts in $\frac{3}{4}$ time } for a whole measure

The Desert Song

Echo Rock

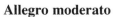

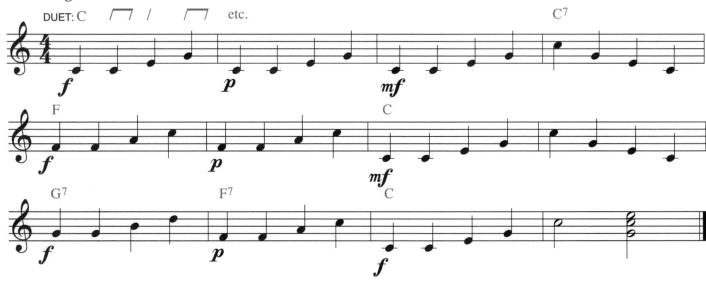

FOUR-STRING C CHORD

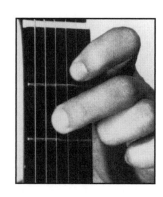
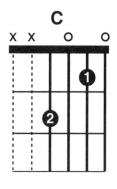

This chord is the first one that uses two fingers at the same time. Finger the three-string C chord, and also place your second finger on the 2nd fret of the 4th string.

TIES

A *tie* is a curved line that joins two or more notes of the same pitch. When two notes are tied, the second is not played separately, but its value is instead added to the first note.

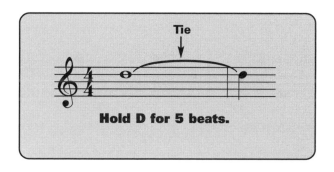

Shenandoah

When the Saints Go Marching In (duet or trio*)

Moderato

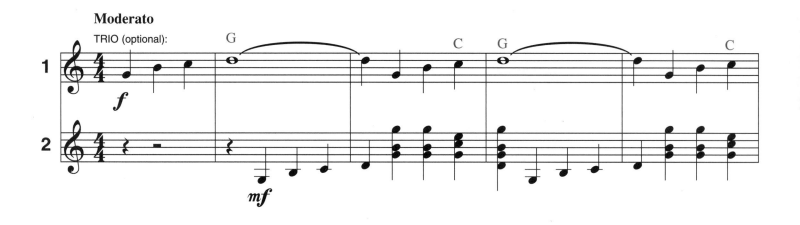

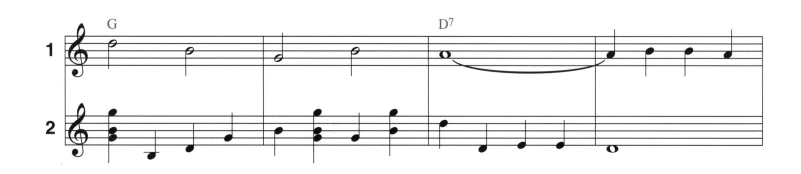

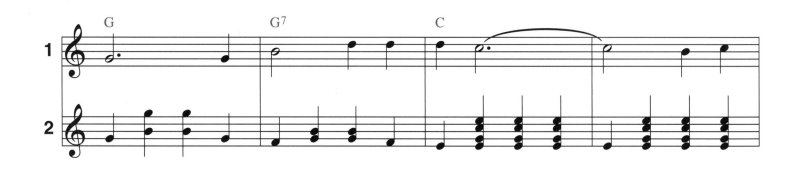

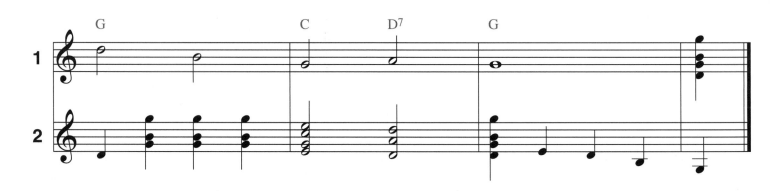

*A *trio* is performed by three players.

Guitar Fingerboard Chart

Frets 1–12

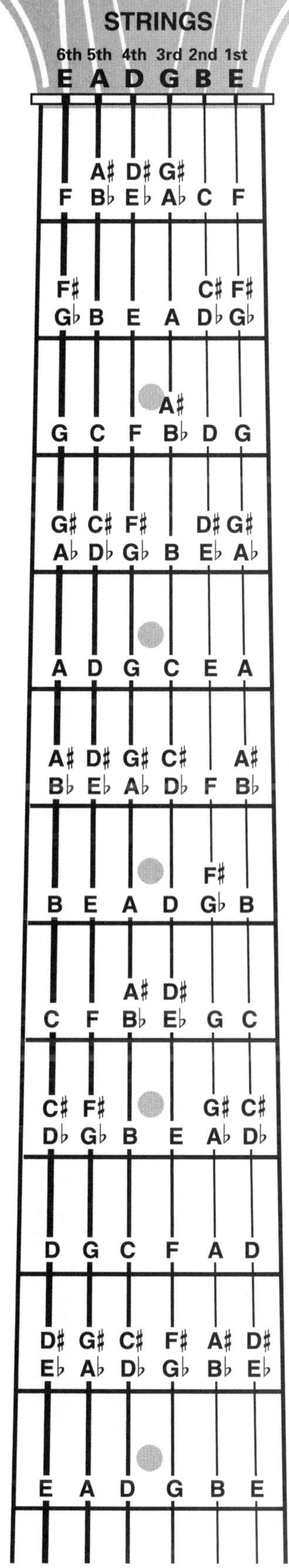

FRETS	6th	5th	4th	3rd	2nd	1st
Open	E	A	D	G	B	E
1st Fret	F	A♯/B♭	D♯/E♭	G♯/A♭	C	F
2nd Fret	F♯/G♭	B	E	A	C♯/D♭	F♯/G♭
3rd Fret	G	C	F	A♯/B♭	D	G
4th Fret	G♯/A♭	C♯/D♭	F♯/G♭	B	D♯/E♭	G♯/A♭
5th Fret	A	D	G	C	E	A
6th Fret	A♯/B♭	D♯/E♭	G♯/A♭	C♯/D♭	F	A♯/B♭
7th Fret	B	E	A	D	F♯/G♭	B
8th Fret	C	F	A♯/B♭	D♯/E♭	G	C
9th Fret	C♯/D♭	F♯/G♭	B	E	G♯/A♭	C♯/D♭
10th Fret	D	G	C	F	A	D
11th Fret	D♯/E♭	G♯/A♭	C♯/D♭	F♯/G♭	A♯/B♭	D♯/E♭
12th Fret	E	A	D	G	B	E

CERTIFICATE OF PROMOTION

This certifies that

has mastered and perfected
Alfred's MAX™ Guitar 1
and is hereby promoted to
Alfred's MAX™ Guitar 2.

Teacher

Date